BORN AGAIN
SELF

A SECOND CHANCE TO FLY HIGHER

ANN MARIE JACKSON

BORN AGAIN SELF

A Second Chance To Fly Higher

MOTIVATION AND MINDSET SHIFT

BORN AGAIN SELF
ANN MARIE JACKSON

Paperback book - ISBN: 978-1-7772126-8-1
Ebook - ISBN: 978-1-7772126-7-4

INTRODUCTION

YOU Are Bigger
Than This Prison

From the day you were born, you entered into a
prison, "A Prison of the MIND".

Born in a room filled with strangers in uniforms,
who were excited to welcome you into this world,
the Land of the Free.

But are you really free? As a spirit, freedom is your
intent, but as a human being, it is not the experience
you imagined.

You are assigned managers, your parents, who
will control your every move. Teachers, who will
keep you in line with the programs, and the laws of
the land to keep you safe, protected, and in line, as the
lawmakers instructed.

Your parents thought they had a voice in raising you,
but they were wrong.

Their job is to keep you alive, and in line, otherwise,
they can be held accountable for any danger that could
possibly jeopardize your well-being.

BORN AGAIN SELF

We chose our parents before coming to earth.
We also choose our experiences in order to evolve.

We chose them, good or bad, to have these rewarding
experiences living on this planet while discovering
truth, lies, reality and most importantly ourselves.

Every person in your life is an assigned angel that God
summoned to protect and guide you along your journey.

Our heartbreaks, disappointments, abuse, neglect,
bullying, abandonment and so many other issues we
encountered throughout life, came upon us so that we
will become one with **Grace, Forgiveness, Love** and
most importantly, true self- identity.

In the end, the prize will be **Agape Love** that exudes
Peace, Love, Joy, and **Happiness.**

All of the knowledge you deemed important, from
your ABC to your PhD has been programming.
Welcome to your new reality.

Today, I can say that I am free of the programming. I
live among it, but I am not a part of it. I am grateful
for my awakening, my true identity on this earth,
which is love.

Through it all, I discovered myself, and today I am free
to forgive my past, and freely give and receive love.

Live through the spirit within, not the flesh.
Your spirit is God, and all of your guidance and
knowledge comes from Him.

Our spirit is free to live, and enjoy life, but our minds are held hostage through a system designed to program. Release the programming. Free yourself.

God is not impressed by your degrees. I promise you he is not saying, "Well done my child" when you graduate with high honors. You are fulfilling a human desire, based on the program. Ask yourself the question, who I'm I really thanking for my earthly accomplishments?

Live through the spirit and the spirit will live through you. Awaken, and live your best life that is freedom.

I trust that the humble realizations in this book will inspire you to reflect on your own personal journey and forgive all the players on your team. The ones who helped you reclaim your true identity by enforcing pain to your experiences, while realizing that there was always an assigned angel at your side to lift you out of your darkness.

Now claim your true identity, which is **extraordinary**. Claim these affirmations and awaken to who you were destined to be.

You are who you say you are, and who you are and have always been, is **FREE!**

About the Author

Ann Marie Jackson is an International Relationship Coach, Master Matchmaker, Author and self-described " Divine Feminine". As a woman of stature and all woman, Ms. Jackson's experiences have been experiential, God-inspired and evolutionary. Her unique approach to empowering her client's focuses on getting them to understand the real meaning of love for their better lives. She has more than 20 years of experience counseling and coaching individuals who were in, between or out of dysfunctional relationships. Her first of four forthcoming books, **"Love: Sacred as an Orgasm,"** Finding **genuine love** in an **over sexualized society",** provides practical strategies to establish and maintain healthy relationships and how to safely extinguish toxic ones. Through her school, Connect Me Academy, Ms. Jackson will further promote healthy relationships that endure the test of time and trial through her workbooks, workshops, online courses, seminars, webinars, and retreats. As she refines her message of healing to individuals, couples and their families, her approach will evolve according to constructive feedback from her clients. The growth and development of client feedback and testimonies will constantly be reflected in new, improved, and repaired relationships. The divine guidance of God and the collective wisdom Ms. Jackson will gain on this journey will strip lies and masks from the unhappy and nonproductive nature that seems to characterize many of today's relationships. As the messenger, Ms. Jackson only requires that anyone embrace the concepts in her book, academy and associated enterprises as the validation to a healthier and longer life and relationships.

Your ABC Bible
Who are you?
I am who I say I am!

A

1

I am an earth ANGEL

2

I will be ACCOUNTABLE for my experiences in this life

3

I am truly an AWESOME Person inside and out

4

I am ABLE to discern right from wrong

5

I am ALWAYS looking for the good in other people

6

I APPRECIATE my body for letting me know that I am not aligned

7

I live for AGAPE love

B

8

I see BEAUTY in everyone and in everything I see and touch

9

I am BLESSED and highly favored by my Creator and life

10

*I am BRAVE and not afraid of
what lies ahead of me*

11

I go BOLDLY into my destiny

12

**My BLESSINGS come from one source;
It is God.**

13

Life is a BREATHTAKING event

14

Daily I am BLOSSOMING into my Best-self

C

15

I CAST *all my cares away*

16

I am CONFIDENT in who I am

17

I CONGRATULATE myself from where I've come

18

My CREATIVE *ability is no longer dormant in me*

19

I no longer need to be CORRECT.
I choose peace.

20

I CELEBRATE *life everyday,*
because tomorrow is not promised.

21

I am CLEAR about who I am

22

Love is a CHOICE, and I choose it

23

I am CHOSEN to be here

D

24

I am no longer a DREAMER;
I am a DOER

25

I am DEPENDENT on no man.
God is my source.

26

*I am enjoying life's journey
as I DISCOVER myself*

27

I am a DIVINE Feminine Boss

28

I DARE you to be you

29

I am totally DEVOTED to loving myself

30

I now DANCE to the rhythm of my own life

32

I DETACH myself from negativity

33

I am DETERMINE to give the
love that I DESERVE

E

34

I am selective with whom I share my ENERGY

35

I am ENJOYING this journey called life

36

I am ENOUGH

37

I am *EQUALLY* gifted, *EQUIPPED* and *EVENTFUL* as the person next door.

38

My Self-ESTEEM is on one hundred

39

I am EVOLVING into a beautiful butterfly

40

It is important to be an EXAMPLE in my community

41

I am **EXCITED** about my journey and
the people who helped me to grow

42

I EXUDE beauty, joy and
abundance in my life.

F

43

I have FAITH in my creator

44

I am FULL of hope

45

I am FREE to love and be loved

46

I am a FRIEND to myself before
I am a friend to others

47

I am FUNNY at times. I love laughter

48

*I recognize the importance of **FORGIVENESS**. It's for my peace of mind*

49

My FUTURE is rich in possibilities

50

Life is not FAIR at times, but is it is always FAVORABLE in the end

G

51

I recognize the GENIUS in me

52

I am so GRATEFUL for my accomplishments, and the people who stood by my side.

53

God has been extremely GOOD to me

54

I am GLAD to be alive

55

I recognize the GODDESS in me

56

I have GROWN so much spiritually

57

My spirit is free of GUILT for
being true to me

H

58

I am a spirit of God having a
HUMAN *experience*

59

My goal in life is to be HAPPY

60

I love receiving HUGS

61

I allow my life to flow with the
HARMONY *of life itself*

62

My HEALING comes from within, not from without

63

Why is HONESTY such a lonely word

64

HUMILITY resides in my DNA

65

My true hero lives within me

I

66

**I trust my life have been IMPACTFUL
to the lives I've touched**

67

It is IMPERATIVE to live my best life

68

My goal in life is not to IMPRESS but to INSPIRE

69

I live with INTEGRITY

70

INTIMACY, Into me see

72

I am IMMORTAL

73

**My presence ILLUMINES light
onto this planet**

74

I strive for INNER-PEACE

J
75

I feel JOY and contentment in my heart

76

I am a JEWEL in Gods' eye

77

I JUSTIFY nothing

80

I won the JACKPOT the day I was born

81

**There is no need to be JEALOUS,
*I am the prize***

82

This **JOURNEY** called life is truly eye opening and I appreciate every moment.

K

83

I am a **KIND-HEARTED** human being
enjoying my life experiences

84

Inside of me, there is a KID who loves to play

85

I believe in KARMA

86

I am my brother's KEEPER

87

I am the KEYNOTE speaker of my life

88

My KNOWLEDGE of self have made me powerful beyond measure

89

My love LANGUAGE is Acts Of Kindness

90

I am the LOVE that I need

91

I am the LIGHT of this world,
I feel LIBERATED

92

My LOYALTY is with God

93

**Because the spirit of God LIVES,
tomorrow is promised**

M

94

It's a **MAGICAL** time to be alive

95

It is MANIFESTATION *season* for *those who have been obedient*

96

I am a MASTERPIECE

97

Prayer is where I talk to God,
MEDITATION is where I listen.

98

MONEY *creates opportunities for* **MYSELF** *and others*

99

Self MASTERY is the key to my success.

N

100

I am generally a NICE person

101

*Saying "NO" and meaning
it is my protection*

102

NO weapon formed against me shall prosper

103

NEVER *say* NEVER.

104

---

*I am no longer NAÏVE in my
relationships with friendships or romance*

105

The NAKED truth will always set me free

106

I find it **NECESSARY** to set boundaries in my relationships.

107

I am excited for my NEXT Chapter POST-COVID

O

108

I am ONE Hundred Percent
in love with life

109

I am ONE-OF-A-KIND

110

I am OFFICIALLY *in alignment with my soul's purpose*

111

I am OBLIGATED to no one but God.

112

My love for life and people is ONGOING

P

113

It is very important to PRAY. PRAYER changes your situation

114

PEOPLE need PEOPLE

116

**I take my PARENTAL
responsibilities very serious**

117

I am **PASSIONATE** about my chosen profession

118

I choose PEACE all day, and all night long

Q

119

QUEEN resides in my DNA

120

I am on a QUEST to mastering self-love

122

*My **QUALITY-TIME** with self is a breath of fresh air for me*

123

Positive QUOTES and affirmations
helps my mind stay fit

R

124

In life, you REAP whatever you sow

125

RECONCILE with
yourself when you are losing.

126

Self-REFLECTION is important for personal growth

127

REJOICE *and give thanks today and every day of your life*

128

REJUVENATE *your spirit daily with positive thoughts, and people*

S

129

---

*I enjoy sharing a **SMILE** with unfamiliar faces*

130

SHARING *is caring*

131

You are divinely SAFE in the arms of your creator

132

I am no longer a SLAVE to my past

133

I am **SECURE** *in who I am.*

T

134

Your TALENT is your gift.
Your gift is your money maker

135

**Mind your THOUGHTS,
they create THINGS**

136

We are united TOGETHER in spirit

137

---

*I am the **TREASURE** you seek*

138

TRUST *your intuition, it is God speaking*

U

139

**Your life is UNFOLDING daily,
*pay attention***

140

*There is **UNLIMITED** abundance in the Universe awaiting you*

141

UTILIZE *your gifts for profit*

142

UNCONDITIONAL is the only true love.
It has no conditions

V

143

VALUE *your friendships that are genuine*

144

VICTORY *is mine today*

145

VENGEANCE belong to God

146

I am a VALUABLE asset to my earthly team

147

I am a VETERAN in this game of love

W

148

A WISE man once said, Be Still.

149

Your WORDS can never harm me

150

The WAY to my heart is good vibes

151

No **WEAPON** *formed against
me shall prosper*

152

My WISH for you is love, joy, happiness and peace of mind

Y

153

I say YES to life

155

I shall be forever YOUNG at heart

156

I YELL to the mountaintop that I am love

I AM FREE

CONNECT WITH ANN MARIE JACKSON

Connect Me Academy

www.ConnectMeAcademy.com

Email ConnectMeAcademy@gmail.com.com

Social media LINKS
https://www.facebook.com/connectmeacademy/
https://twitter.com/connectmacademy
https://www.linkedin.com/in/ann-jackson-8a372118/
https://www.instagram.com/connectmeacademy/

www.ingramcontent.com/pod-product-compliance
Lightning Source LLC
Chambersburg PA
CBHW051115050726
47592CB00002B/834